Fixing Hubble's Troubles

by Philip Stewart

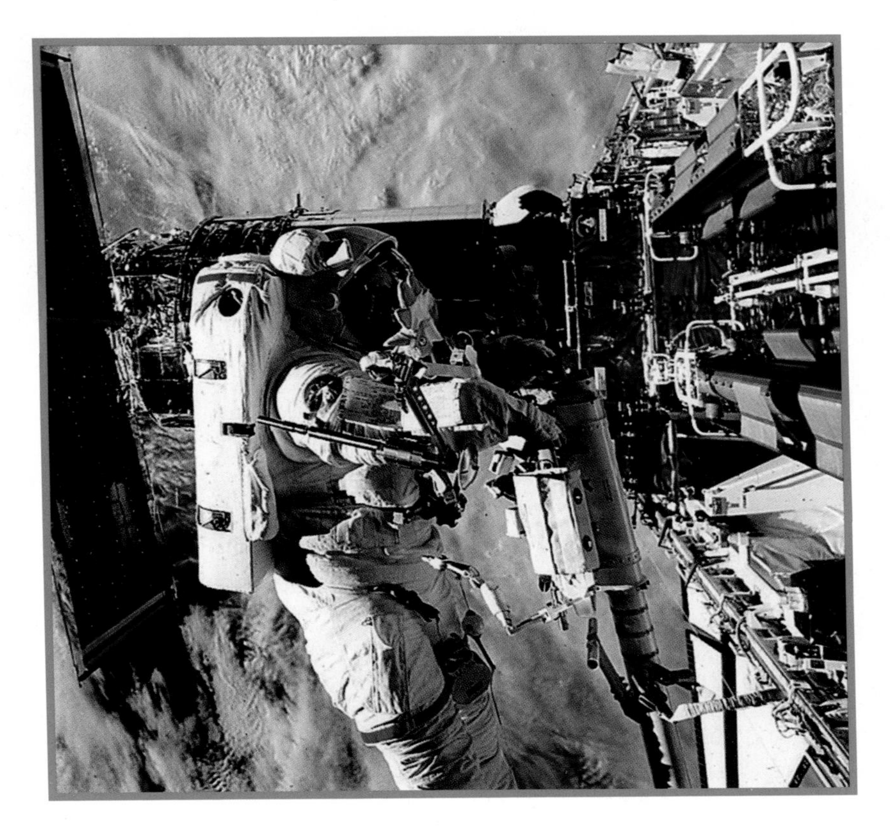

Glenview, Illinois • Boston, Massachusetts • Chandler, Arizona
Upper Saddle River, New Jersey

The Hubble Space Telescope

The Hubble Space Telescope

Scientists study the sky with telescopes. These are tools to make things look closer. But scientists could not see things in space clearly. They needed better telescopes.

Scientists wanted to put a telescope in space. It would travel around Earth. It would send clear pictures of space.

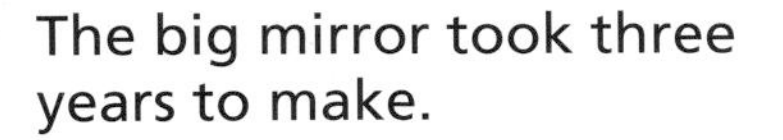
The big mirror took three years to make.

In 1990, *Discovery* carried Hubble into space.

Scientists made the Hubble Space Telescope. Hubble was as big as a school bus! Its mirror was eight feet wide. Hubble had cameras. It had other tools too. It used them to send information to Earth.

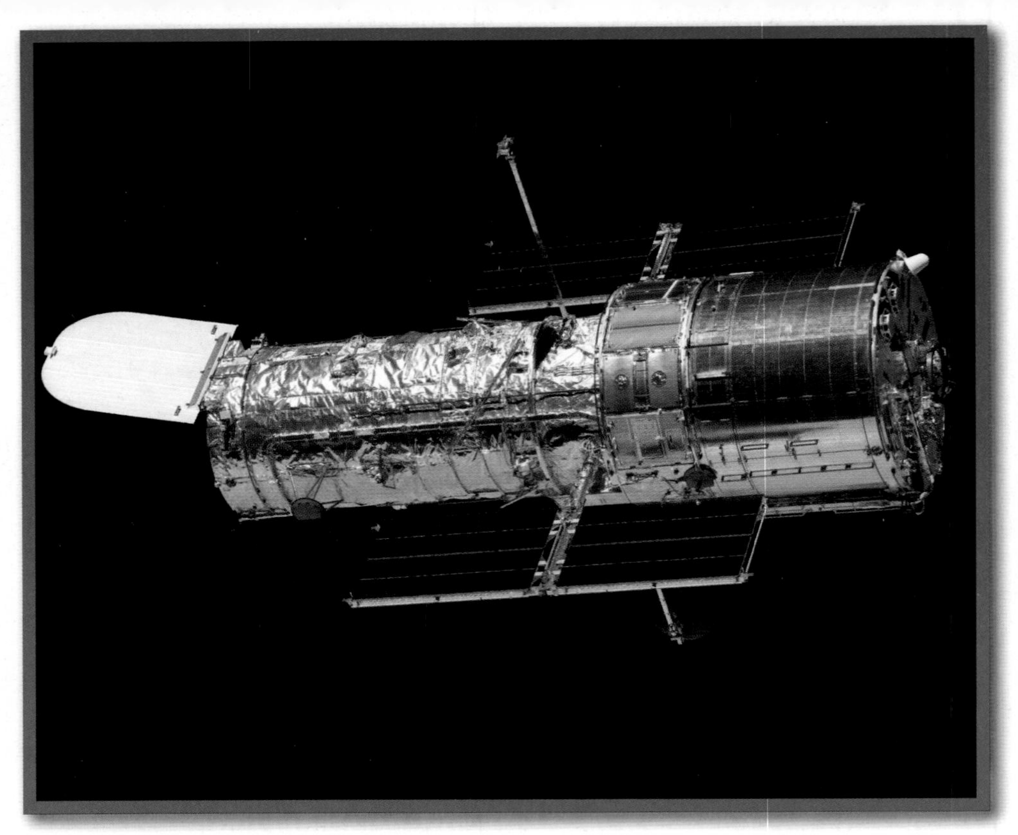

This is Hubble.

Soon, scientists were worried. Hubble was not sending clear pictures. Scientists found the problem. The most important mirror was wrong. It was not the right shape. They needed to fix it.

They could not put in a new mirror. So they made a tool. It would make Hubble's pictures clear. This tool worked just like glasses.

Fixing a telescope in space is hard. Astronauts would have to go into space. It would be a special mission. They had a big job.

Extend Language **A Multiple-Meaning Word**

Missions can be buildings. They are places where people do work to help others.

A *mission* can also be "a special trip to do an important job." The astronauts who fixed Hubble were on a mission.

Space Repairs

Scientists knew Hubble would need to be fixed over time. So they made Hubble in a special way. The telescope had handrails.

But Hubble would be hard to fix. Scientists picked the best astronauts to do the job. The astronauts went to space in the shuttle *Endeavour* in 1993.

Astronauts can hold the handrails when they fix Hubble.

The astronauts of the first repair mission: (top, left to right) Richard Covey, Jeffrey Hoffman, Thomas Akers, (bottom, left to right) Kenneth Bowersox, Kathryn Thornton, Story Musgrave, Claude Nicollier.

The seven astronauts trained for a year. Each member had a special job:

- **Richard Covey** was the commander. He was in charge.
- **Ken Bowersox** was the pilot. He flew the shuttle.
- **Claude Nicollier** moved the robotic arm. This is a special tool. It carried the astronauts and their tools.
- **Story Musgrave** was the payload commander. He planned the walks out in space to fix Hubble.
- **Jeffrey Hoffman, Thomas Akers,** and **Kathryn Thornton** fixed the telescope.

Hubble was put in the *Endeavour*'s payload bay.

It took two days to reach Hubble. Once the *Endeavour* got there, Claude Nicollier grabbed Hubble. He used the robotic arm. He put the telescope into the payload bay. This was a garage-like space in the *Endeavour*. There, the astronauts worked on Hubble.

First, Story Musgrove and Jeffrey Hoffman fixed Hubble. They took off broken parts. They put in new parts. Then Thomas Akers and Kathryn Thornton went out. They put in more new parts.

Astronaut Kathryn Thornton works on Hubble.

Astronaut Jeffrey Hoffman takes off the old camera.

Next, Story Musgrove and Jeffrey Hoffman put on a new camera. This was a hard job. The camera could have broken. They had to be very careful.

Kathryn Thornton lifts the metal box. The box has mirrors in it.

Then Kathryn Thornton and Thomas Akers put in new mirrors. The mirrors would help Hubble send clear pictures. The box of mirrors was big! It was hard for the astronauts to move it around.

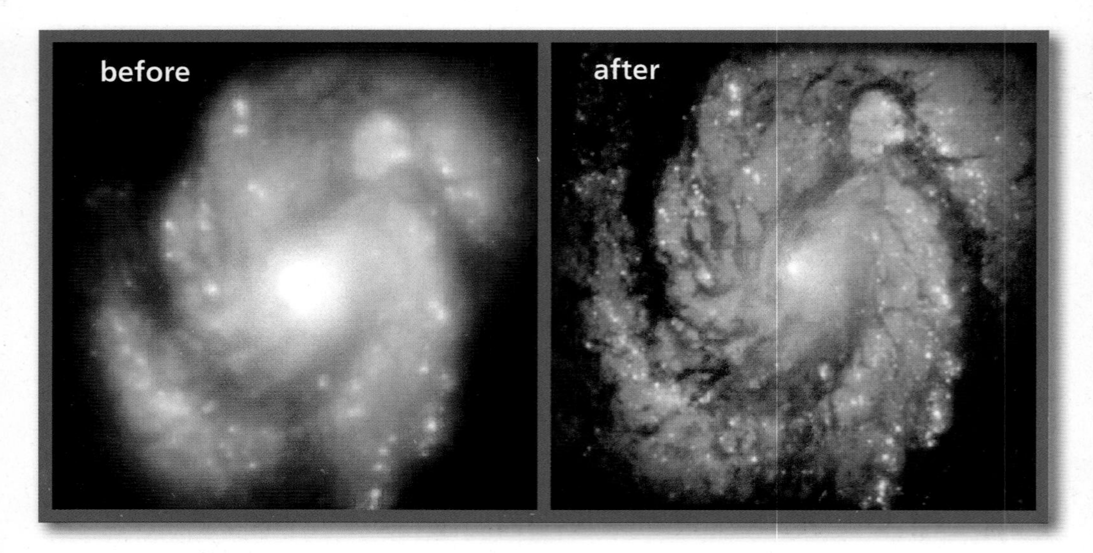

Hubble's pictures were clear after the astronauts fixed it.

Last, Story Musgrove and Jeffrey Hoffman checked everything. Hubble was fixed.

The astronauts put Hubble back in space. Then they went home. They had been in space for ten days.

Scientists were very happy! Hubble sent back clear pictures. The astronauts did a good job.